Anita Benarde

The International Design Library®

Mediterranean Mosaic Designs

Stemmer House

PUBLISHERS, INC.

Owings Mills, Maryl

To Mel—one who appreciates

INTRODUCTION

If an art form were to be singled out for the dubious award of least appreciated, mosaics would "win in a walk." It is the rare historian of art who can even name an artist of this medium. And though originality often sets art apart from craft, classical mosaics—among the most original of artistic creations—are often categorized as mere craft. Fortunately, in 1963 an international conference of scholars was convened in Paris to explore means of rectifying what was seen as deplorable neglect.

Even the origin of the word "mosaic" is uncertain. While some historians have suggested an Arabic derivation, it is clear that mosaic was not an arabic invention. More likely is its relationship to the Muses—"Mousaikon"—the nine Greek Goddesses, patrons of the arts and sciences, which suggests that the technique was in fact associated with the highest forms of artistic expression.

But just what is it? To be all-encompassing, the definition must be broad, as for example, "a design, a coherent pattern, built up by the application of thousands of small pieces of ceramic, stone, marble, glass and/or shell of roughly uniform shape, size and thickness, and held to flat or curved surfaces by a plaster-like material."

It would be just as correct to say simply that Mosaic is the art of decorating a surface with designs made up of closely set, multicolored pieces of stone, glass, ceramic, shell or marble.

Among the earliest forms of mosaic were the black-and-white pebble mosaics used as flooring of buildings in Athens, Delphi and Olympus. Black was used for background and the white for figures and patterns: at times dark red, green, gray and purple pebbles were also used. Some of the earliest date from 400 B.C.

During the Hellenistic period (4th to 1st centuries B.C.) the simpler designs developed into the form continued into the modern period. With the introduction of regularly shaped tesserae of roughly uniform size, not only was a finish possible, but opportunities for a higher esthetic content were increased.

A distinction is also made between two types—amounting to separate media: the floor mosaic of the classical period (Greece and Rome) and the wall mosaic prevalent in the middle ages.

Because it will be walked on, a floor mosaic had to be firm and smooth both in material and in fitting; and as it would be seen from eye-level there was scope for a display of intricate detail. On the other hand, a wall or ceiling design, not being exposed to physical punishment, could be of less robust materials, and did not require a smooth surface. Consequently the pieces could be set at differing angles and planes.

Important, too, was the fact that a mosaic required laborious assembly of thousands of tiny colored fragments—which first had to be found and cut—making the process an unusually expensive one, requiring rich patrons. This severely limited its use and distribution. Nevertheless, elegant examples have been found as far apart as Syria in the East, Spain in the West, and all the way from North Africa to as far north as Kiev.

Of course mosaics have an advantage over other media, such as painting, in that it can resist and survive the decay and disintegration wrought by time. Paintings often bleach out, or color relations become altered: frescoes are subject to attack by mold, or they flake off. Mosaics, however, survive intact with the same vivid colors given them by the original artist. They appear to be perennially fresh and vital. They are, as has been pointed out, "true paintings for all eternity."

Commesso (derived from the Latin past participle of the verb *commettere,* meaning "put together" or "joined") is an especially graceful form of mosaic. The process, developed in sixteenth-century Florence, was used primarily for table tops and small wood panels. It has special features which result from the emphasis upon choice of colors,

and detail can be reproduced with such exquisite precision as to rival paintings in their realism. The artists designed pictures using thin, cut-to-shape pieces of hard colored stones—chalcedony, jasper, agate, transparent amethyst and lapis lazuli. All except lapis are hard stones—falling between feldspar and diamond in hardness.

Florentine commesso developed under Francesco I as a prelude to the construction of the Medici chapel. The quality of the work owes a great deal to the skills of gem-cutting which had been practiced for centuries under the Medicis.

Such artists as Bernardo Buontalente, Malteo Negetti, Jacopo Ligozzi and Ludovico Cardo were responsible for developing and spreading a taste for colored stones, and they also developed the art of pictorial design which gave the illusion of perspective.

At the time, the greatest need was to discover the colors that lay hidden in mountain and river bed stones. They were so desirable that the Grand Duke Ferdinando offered prizes for finding the stones and ordered punishment for anyone who wastefully scattered them.

From examples seen in the Prado Museum in Madrid, it is obvious that commesso artists did not use only the small square tesserae of the traditional mosaics. Instead they sliced the gemstones to achieve specific shapes and sizes. In addition, the natural lines of the stones were used to obtain painterly effects.

Intarsia, often translated as "inlay," is another variation of mosaic art. Although intarsia, commesso and mosaic are similar and can easily be mistaken for one another, true intarsia requires that the base material into which the design is inlaid be an essential element in the resulting decorative effect.

Apparently two major types have been developed—wood and stone. Inlaid wood seems to have been the province of the artists in the monastic orders of Northern Italy, who used the technique to decorate church furniture. Secular artists appeared to dominate stone intarsia, which found its greatest expression as floors in churches and private villas.

With the appearance in the eleventh and twelfth centuries of cosmatine or cosmati work, as it was often called, floor mosaics had a renaissance in the Western world. Cosmati work required small and triangular units that were repeated endlessly to form primarily star-like patterns. The pieces were made from red porphory, green serpentine and white colored marble.

Cosmatine derives its name from the Cosma family of Florence, a dynasty of architect-decorators. These artists also used gold leaf sandwiched between pieces of glass, which produced brilliant highlights and reflections. Cosmati mosaics were used as floor coverings or pavements in order to achieve brilliance indoors when light played on their surfaces.

Mosaics, whatever their form, deserve greater appreciation and understanding.

However, a definite revival is occurring. This renaissance was led by Antoni Gaudi (Spain), Georges Braque (France), Marc Chagall (U.S./Israel), David Siqueiros and Diego Rivera (Mexico) and Hans Erni (Berne). It owes much also to the establishment of the INIASA School in Venice and the Instituto Statale D'Arte per il Mosaico, in Ravenna—an art school with special emphasis on mosaics. Both have been instrumental in developing masters of this art form.

It may be of interest to learn that the designs included in this collection have been created with minimal use of rulers or templates. Brushes and pens were used for the most part, since the concern here was to convey the free-hand feeling of the originals.

A.B.

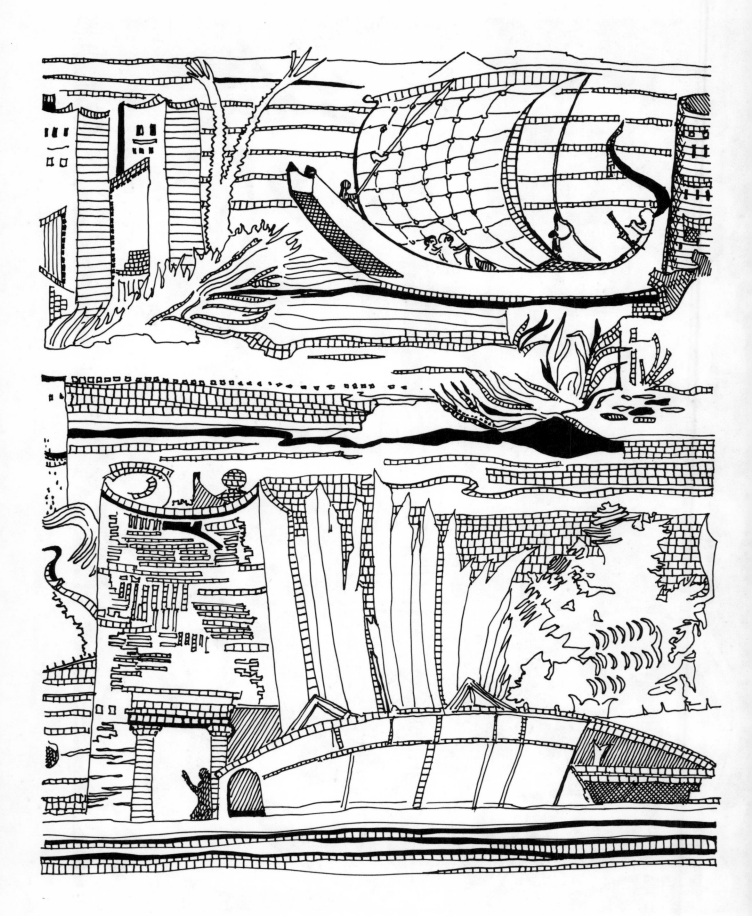

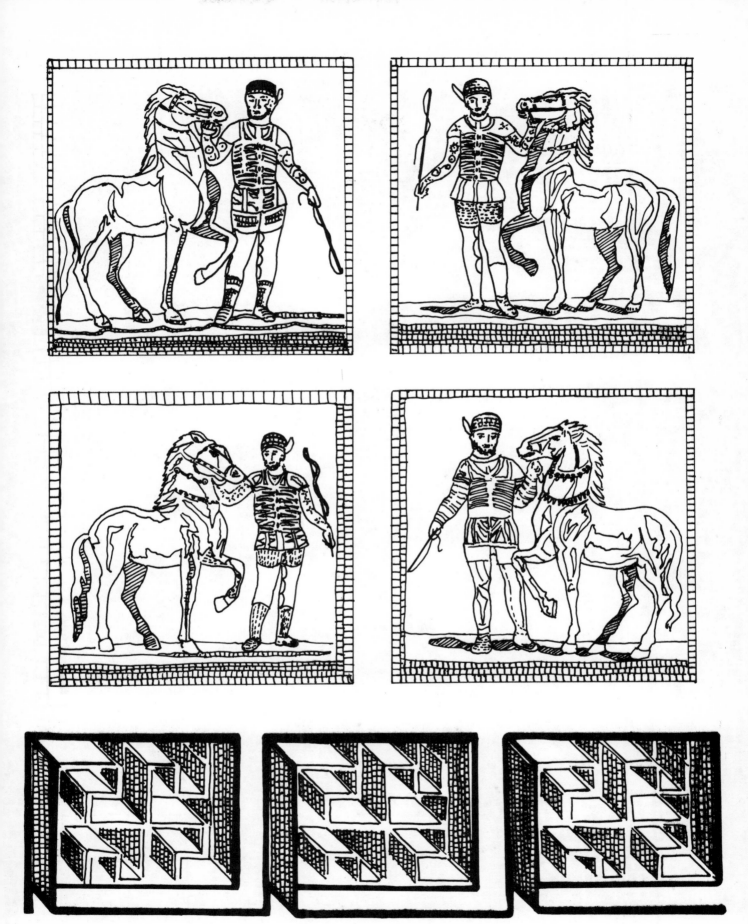

Designed by Barbara Holdridge
Composed by BG Composition, Inc.,
        Baltimore, Maryland
Cover printed by Strine Printing Co., Inc.,
        York, Pennsylvania
Printed and bound by Port City Press, Inc.,
        Baltimore Maryland
        on 75-pound Williamsburg Offset